M257 Unit 7
UNDERGRADUATE COMPUTING
Putting Java to work

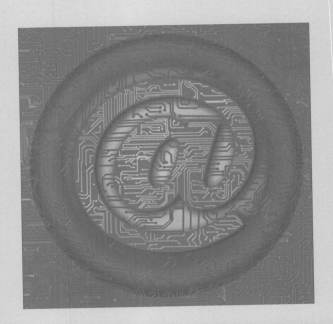

Event-driven
programming

Unit 7

This publication forms part of an Open University course M257 *Putting Java to work*. Details of this and other Open University courses can be obtained from the Student Registration and Enquiry Service, The Open University, PO Box 197, Milton Keynes MK7 6BJ, United Kingdom: tel. +44 (0)870 333 4340, email general-enquiries@open.ac.uk

Alternatively, you may visit the Open University website at http://www.open.ac.uk where you can learn more about the wide range of courses and packs offered at all levels by The Open University.

To purchase a selection of Open University course materials visit http://www.ouw.co.uk, or contact Open University Worldwide, Michael Young Building, Walton Hall, Milton Keynes MK7 6AA, United Kingdom for a brochure. tel. +44 (0)1908 858785; fax +44 (0)1908 858787; email ouwenq@open.ac.uk

The Open University
Walton Hall, Milton Keynes
MK7 6AA

First published 2007. Second edition 2008.

Edited, designed and typeset by The Open University.

Printed and bound in the United Kingdom by Hobbs the Printers Ltd, Totton, Hampshire.

ISBN 978 0 7492 1992 5

2.1

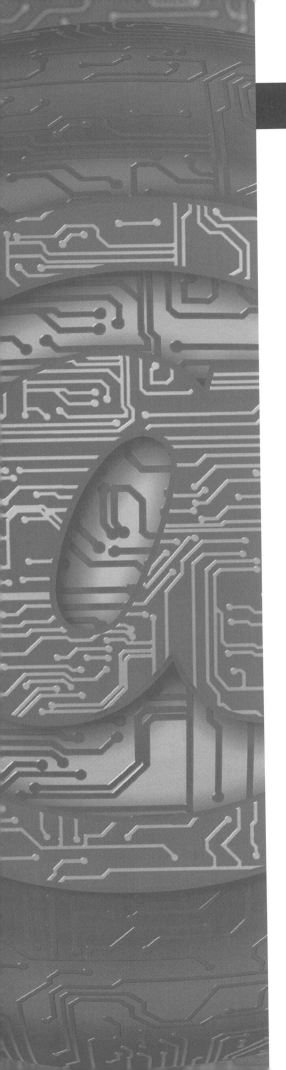

CONTENTS

M257 COURSE TEAM

M257 *Putting Java to work* was adapted from M254 *Java everywhere*.

M254 was produced by the following team.

Martin Smith, Course Team Chair and Author

Anton Dil, Author

Brendan Quinn, Author

Janet Van der Linden, Academic Editor

Barbara Poniatowska, Course Manager

Ralph Greenwell, Course Manager

Alkis Stavrinides, External Assessor, Coventry University

Critical readers

Pauline Curtis, Associate Lecturer

David Knowles, Associate Lecturer

Robin Walker, Associate Lecturer

Richard Walker, Associate Lecturer

The M257 adaptation was produced by:

Darrel Ince, Course Team Chair and Author

Richard Walker, Consultant Author and Critical Reader

Matthew Nelson, Critical Reader

Barbara Poniatowska, Course Manager

Ralph Greenwell, Course Manager

Alkis Stavrinides, External Assessor, Coventry University

Media development staff

Andrew Seddon, Media Project Manager

Garry Hammond, Editor

Ian Blackham, Editor

Anna Edgley-Smith, Editor

Jenny Brown, Freelance Editor

Andrew Whitehead, Designer and Graphic Artist

Glen Derby, Designer

Phillip Howe, Compositor

Lisa Hale, Compositor

Thanks are due to the Desktop Publishing Unit of the Faculty of Mathematics and Computing.

1 Introduction

The previous unit, *Unit 6*, has shown you how to create graphical user interfaces that contain a wide range of components and have quite sophisticated layouts. You are also in a position now to make use of Java reference material to investigate and use other components and layouts. However, when the user clicks on a button or enters text, nothing happens. This is because there is no link between the graphical user interface and the code that you would like to be executed.

Creating this link between something happening in the graphical user interface – an **event** – and the execution of code is the subject of this unit. This subject is commonly known as **event-driven programming**. Event-driven programs are programs that respond to events initiated by the user, such as mouse clicks and key presses. Events can also be initiated through software coding, using for example the `Timer` class, which may specify that certain events are to take place at certain times. However, this course will consider only user-initiated events.

Event-driven programming represents an entirely different style of programming. All of the code that you have worked on so far has been fairly 'linear' in nature – it has been possible to plot a route through the code to show the order of execution. However, with event-driven programming this is no longer necessarily the case. Essentially, components are waiting around for an outside body – the user – to initiate an event through one of the visual components – clicking a button, for example. But you, the programmer, do not know *when* the button will be pressed, whether a *number of buttons* will be pressed, or in *which order* the user will press them.

You will see that a major part of event-driven programming is the creation of objects called listeners that are attached to components. As their name suggests they 'listen' for events happening to 'their' components. These listeners then 'fire' off the desired code. Listeners can be 'told' to look at particular components and to look only at particular events. For example, a listener may be interested only in a mouse entering a particular part of the screen and not in it being clicked.

We will also continue with the `Calculator` example started in the last unit. In this unit we show how the action of the user clicking on a button can be linked to the code that will carry out the actions and then display the result.

In this unit, we aim to:

▶ introduce event-driven programming;

▶ show how to link external events to program code;

▶ introduce the `Graphics` class and simple animation;

▶ give you an overall view of the construction of working GUIs through a number of fully developed examples.

2 The Swing event system

In *Unit 6*, we dealt with the problem of creating and displaying visual objects such as buttons and text areas. The major remaining topic that we need to look at is how such objects respond to events. Typical events that can be generated in a computer system are:

▶ a button being clicked;

▶ a text field being modified;

▶ a menu being accessed;

▶ a list element being selected.

This unit describes how to program Java code so that when events such as those above occur, some processing takes place. The processing may affect visual objects or it may be some internal processing such as the calculation of a value.

2.1 Overview of event handling

In order to describe how events are handled, two small items of vocabulary need to be introduced. An **event source** is an object that gives rise to an event. Typical event sources are buttons and menu lists. An event **listener** is an object that responds to an event. So the source of the event and the place where the event is dealt with are separate. This nicely separates the interface (the visual components) from the implementation (the code that carries out the processing). If, at a later date, either the graphical user interface or the processing code has to change then these changes can be localized.

The actual sequence of events that happens is quite involved. The button click, for example, is picked up by the operating system of the computer and is passed to the Java Virtual Machine. The message is then passed through a number of levels before ending up with the visual components.

When an event happens to a component of the visual interface, that component reports the event to the 'system'. If you are interested in that event (for example, a mouse click on a button), then you will register your interest by attaching an event listener for that particular action to that particular component. If you are not interested in that event (for example, a mouse simply moving over a button) then you do not attach an event listener and the event will not be acted upon when it occurs.

Each event listener is an object of a class that implements a specific type of listener interface (note that this is an interface in the Java programming sense). Inside the listener you put the code that triggers off the processing that you want to happen when an event occurs.

So in order to get a visual component that 'does something', you need to follow a three-step plan.

1 Create and place the component on the graphical user interface.

2 Define the required event listener class.

3 Create an instance of the event listener and register it with the component.

The first of these three steps was the subject of *Unit 6*.

2.2 Capturing an event from a button

We will start by looking at the intuitively simple example of a button being clicked. This also turns out to be one of the simplest events to program.

Although there are many events to which you might want a button to respond (such as the mouse passing over it), the main event that you are likely to be interested in is that of the button being clicked by the user. This means that we need to create an object that will sit around waiting for the particular button to be pressed. This object will contain the code that we wish to run when the button is pressed.

To achieve this, we use the `ActionListener` interface. All of the listeners for the various events are in the form of interfaces. The `ActionListener` interface corresponds to a number of events that are generated by visual objects. They include a button being clicked, an item being selected from a list box, a menu item being selected and the `Enter` key being pressed in a text field.

As `ActionListener` is an interface, we need to define a class that implements all of the methods in the interface in order to create a usable object. With the `ActionListener` interface, there is only one method to be implemented: the `actionPerformed` method. This method is the one that will be executed when an event such as a button being clicked occurs.

However, with some listeners there are many methods and we will see later how we can avoid the need to write code for many methods, most of which we might not want to use.

Once we have created our `ActionListener` object, we need to register it with the component to which we want it to 'listen' – in this case, a button. This is achieved using the `addActionListener` method. All components have methods to add and remove listeners from themselves, and the method names follow a fairly simple convention of `add` (or `remove`) followed by the *event* followed by `Listener`. You will see more examples of this later.

The following code shows the above points.

```java
import java.awt.event.*;
import javax.swing.*;

public class MyFrame extends JFrame
{
    private int buttonClicks;
    private JButton button;
    private JLabel output;

    public MyFrame (String s)
    {
        super(s);
        setSize(300, 300);
        buttonClicks = 0;

        button = new JButton("Press Me");
        output = new JLabel("Starting");
        getContentPane().add(button, "West");
        getContentPane().add(output, "East");
```

```
        /* Create an instance of ButtonWatcher and
        register this object listener with the button. */
        button.addActionListener(new ButtonWatcher());
    }

    /* Define the listener class by implementing
    the interface ActionListener. */
    private class ButtonWatcher implements ActionListener
    {
        /* Here is the code which is executed when
        the button is clicked. */
        public void actionPerformed (ActionEvent a)
        {
            buttonClicks++;
            output.setText("" + buttonClicks);
            if (buttonClicks == 10)
            {
                buttonClicks = 0;
            }
        }
    }
}

public class MyFrameTest
{
    public static void main (String[] args)
    {
        MyFrame world = new MyFrame("Button Watcher");
        world.setVisible(true);
    }
}
```

Read through this code carefully, as there are many interesting features about it. We have created a button and a label, placed them in a frame and displayed them through the main method. This is as far as you were able to go in *Unit 6*. Figure 1 shows the screen after a number of button clicks.

Figure 1   The frame **MyFrame** showing a button labelled **Press Me** and a label displaying the number of times the button has been pressed

In order to link the button with some code, we have defined a class of listener called `ButtonWatcher` (it watches our button for events). In the constructor for `MyFrame` we create an instance of `ButtonWatcher` using `new` and then register it with the button to which we want it to listen, using the `addActionListener` method. All this takes place in a single line:

```
button.addActionListener(new ButtonWatcher());
```

The code to define this listener is reproduced below:

```
/* Define the listener class by implementing
the interface ActionListener. */
private class ButtonWatcher implements ActionListener
{
    /* Here is the code which is executed when
    the button is clicked. */
    public void actionPerformed (ActionEvent a)
    {
        buttonClicks++;
        output.setText("" + buttonClicks);
        if (buttonClicks == 10)
        {
            buttonClicks = 0;
        }
    }
}
```

The biggest surprise that you will have had is the fact that this is the definition of a class, `ButtonWatcher`, inside the definition of another class, `MyFrame`. We say that `ButtonWatcher` is an example of an **inner class**.

Inner classes

It is possible to place the definition of one class inside another class definition; this class is then known as an inner class. There are a number of practical and conceptual advantages of doing this. One of the conceptual advantages is that it allows you to keep together classes that are logically related to each other. In the above case we are defining a class that will act as a listener for a button. We could have defined it as an entirely separate class but in a sense the two class definitions go together. So by defining `ButtonWatcher` inside the class in which we create the button that will be using it, we have kept the two together. One of the practical advantages of using inner classes is that the inner class has access to all of the methods and data fields of the surrounding class.

The inner class can be as complicated as you like and it can make use of all of the modifiers that a 'normal' class would use, and so on. We will meet another practical advantage of inner classes in the next section, when we look at adapters. We will see that adapters are inner classes that can inherit in their own right and are not limited to whatever the outside class has already inherited. In earlier units we discussed that multiple inheritance is not allowed in Java, but interfaces provide a way round this limitation. That is, interfaces provide a mechanism for 'inheritance for specification' from more than one class. We see now that inner classes provide another solution, in that they can inherit using `extends` or, as in the example above, using `implements`.

Event programming

The remaining code within MyFrame is simple: it counts the number of times that the button is clicked, displays the count in a label and resets the count back to zero when it reaches ten.

The series of actions that occur with button clicking is as follows.

1   The button is clicked.

2   The Java system picks up this event and interrogates the button about what action listeners are registered with it.

3   It discovers an action listener.

4   The actionPerformed method associated with ButtonWatcher is executed.

> If there is more than one listener attached to an event, then the order in which they are called is not guaranteed.

But notice that there is something quite remarkable happening in this program, something that we have not seen before. Every time that the user clicks the button, the code is executed no matter how many times they click. Yet there are no loops programmed in the code. To get this type of repetitive behaviour up to now you would have had to include some sort of a loop construct statement to get the program to cycle over and over again. However, with event-driven programming this is not needed. The above code has *defined* (in the inner class), *created* (using new ButtonWatcher) and *attached* (addActionListener) a listener to the button. This listener simply sits there waiting to 'fire' when 'its' event happens on 'its' component.

There are some final points worth making about the above code. First, it needs to import javax.swing for the visual object classes; second, it needs to import java.awt. event for the event classes and interfaces; third, although the actionPerformed method has a single ActionEvent argument a, it is not used within the code. This argument contains subsidiary information about the event, which can be used for more complicated processing.

The event argument

The next example shows the use of the event argument.

```java
import javax.swing.*;
import java.awt.event.*;
import java.awt.*;

public class MySecondFrame extends JFrame
{
    private int buttonClicks;
    private JButton buttonUp, buttonDown;
    private JLabel label;

    public MySecondFrame (String s)
    {
        super(s);
        setSize(300, 300);
        buttonClicks = 0;

        buttonUp = new JButton("Press Me Up");
        buttonDown = new JButton("Press Me Down");
        label = new JLabel("Starting");
```

```
        buttonUp.addActionListener(new ButtonWatcher());
        buttonDown.addActionListener(new ButtonWatcher());

        getContentPane().setLayout(new FlowLayout());
        getContentPane().add(buttonUp);
        getContentPane().add(buttonDown);
        getContentPane().add(label);
    }

    /* Define the listener class by implementing
    the interface ActionListener. */
    private class ButtonWatcher implements ActionListener
    {
        /* Here is the code which is executed when
        the button is clicked. */
        public void actionPerformed (ActionEvent a)
        {
            Object buttonPressed = a.getSource();
            if (buttonPressed.equals(buttonUp))
            {
                buttonClicks++;
            }
            if (buttonPressed.equals(buttonDown))
            {
                buttonClicks--;
            }
            label.setText(buttonClicks + "");
        }
    }
}

public class MySecondFrameTest
{
    public static void main (String[] args)
    {
        MySecondFrame world = new MySecondFrame("Two Buttons");
        world.setVisible(true);
    }
}
```

In this example, there are two buttons. The first button increments the integer displayed in the label and the second decrements the integer. Both buttons have the same listener (ButtonWatcher) attached, so when actionPerformed is executed there is a need to determine the source of the event. This is done by invoking the method getSource. This method returns an object and, using the equals method of the Object class, the specific button pressed can be identified and the appropriate code executed. Figure 2 shows the interface after a number of clicks.

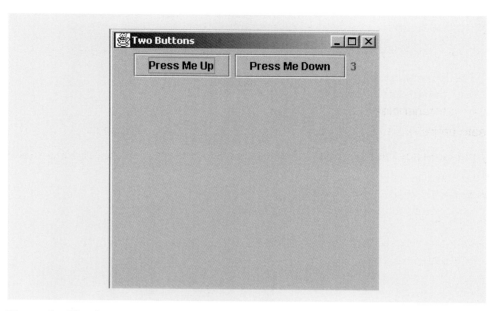

Figure 2   The frame **MySecondFrame** showing two buttons, **Press Me Up** and
Press Me Down, alongside a label showing the current value of **buttonClicks**

2.3   Events in the calculator code

You are now in a position to understand the remainder of the code for the calculator. The
complete program listing is repeated again at the end of this unit. You will see that we
have used the three inner classes KeyPadButtonWatcher,
FunctionButtonWatcher and EqualsButtonWatcher along with the getSource
method to determine the identity of the specific button being pressed. Read through this
code again.

SAQ 1

(a) What is the main difference between event-driven programming and 'normal'
programming?

(b) How do you tell the system that you are interested in knowing when a particular
event has occurred (for example, a button has been clicked)?

(c) What happens if an event occurs that you are not interested in?

ANSWERS ....

(a) With event-driven programming there is no longer a fixed sequence for the
execution of blocks of code. Instead the program reacts to events initiated (usually)
by the user.

(b) You attach the appropriate event listener to the component that you are interested
in.

(c) In that case, nothing happens. Although the system is aware that the event has
taken place, the information is not passed to the program.

SAQ 2

Earlier, it was stated that there were three key steps to producing an interactive graphical user interface:

1 Create the component and add it to the graphical user interface.

2 Define a listener class.

3 Create an instance of the listener and register it with the component.

Identify the three key lines of code that do these three tasks in the class `MyFrame` (see page 7).

ANSWER...

The three steps are as follows.

1 Create the component using `button = new JButton("Press Me")` and place it on the GUI using `getContentPane().add(button, "West")`.

2 Define the listener using `private class ButtonWatcher`, which implements `ActionListener`.

3 Create an instance of the listener and register it with the component using `button. addActionListener(new ButtonWatcher())`.

Activity 7.1
Constructing an interface for font selection.

3 Component listeners

Section 2 introduced you to the concept of listeners through the intuitive example of a button. In this section, we look at the listeners needed for other components and events. You will see that the approach is exactly the same as that with buttons: that is, create the component, define the appropriate listener class and then attach an instance of the listener class to the component. The main complications that arise are due to most listener interfaces being more complex than the `ActionListener`. So, although we will not be able to cover every aspect of all of the events and component combinations, you will have sufficient experience of them to be able to use the Java reference material for the rest.

Table 1 displays a number of events that can be generated by GUI objects.

Table 1 Events generated by GUI objects

Type of event	Associated components
Action events	buttons, lists, menu items and text fields
Adjustment events	scroll bars
Item events	check boxes, choices and lists
Text events	text components such as text fields and text areas
Component events	visual components: for example, being resized or hidden
Container events	containers such as frames: for example, when a component is added or removed
Focus events	components coming into focus or going out of focus
Key events	keys being pressed or released
Mouse events	actions such as clicking a mouse or moving a mouse
Window events	windows: for example, opening or closing a window

The names of the respective listeners are formed by taking the *name of the event* and adding *listener*, so we have `ComponentListener`, `KeyListener` and so on. The `add` and `remove` methods simply have the word *add* (or *remove*) prefixing the interface name, such as `addComponentListener` and `removeKeyListener`.

3.1 Mouse listeners

An important input device when using a graphical user interface is the mouse: it is used to point with, it can be clicked, it can 'drag and drop' items, and so on. In Java there are two interfaces that can be used for mouse events: MouseMotionListener and MouseListener. The former defines two events concerned with dragging and moving the mouse. However, we will concentrate on the second interface, the MouseListener, which defines five methods that are used for monitoring:

▶ when a mouse button is clicked

```
public abstract void mouseClicked (MouseEvent m)
```

▶ when a mouse enters a component

```
public abstract void mouseEntered (MouseEvent m)
```

▶ when a mouse exits a component

```
public abstract void mouseExited (MouseEvent m)
```

▶ when a mouse is pressed

```
public abstract void mousePressed (MouseEvent m)
```

▶ when a mouse button is released

```
public abstract void mouseReleased (MouseEvent m)
```

Any listener that wants to react to any of the above events must implement the MouseListener interface, which contains the definition of the above five methods. An example of the use of this interface is shown below:

```
import java.awt.*;
import java.awt.event.*;
import javax.swing.*;

public class MouseFrame extends JFrame
{
    private JLabel yCoordLabel;
    private JLabel xCoordLabel;
    private JPanel c;

    public MouseFrame (String title)
    {
        super(title);
        setSize(300, 300);
        yCoordLabel = new JLabel("");
        xCoordLabel = new JLabel("");
        c = new JPanel();
        c.setBackground(Color.yellow);
        getContentPane().setLayout(new GridLayout(3, 1));
        getContentPane().add(yCoordLabel);
        getContentPane().add(xCoordLabel);
        getContentPane().add(c);
        c.addMouseListener(new MouseWatcher());
    }
```

```
private class MouseWatcher implements MouseListener
{
    public void mouseClicked (MouseEvent e)
    {
        int xCoordinate = e.getX();
        int yCoordinate = e.getY();
        yCoordLabel.setText(yCoordinate + "");
        xCoordLabel.setText(xCoordinate + "");
    }

    public void mouseEntered (MouseEvent e)
    {
    }

    public void mouseReleased (MouseEvent e)
    {
    }

    public void mousePressed (MouseEvent e)
    {
    }

    public void mouseExited (MouseEvent e)
    {
    }
}
}


public class MouseFrameTest
{
    public static void main (String[] args)
    {
        MouseFrame world = new MouseFrame("Mouse Watcher");
        world.setVisible(true);
    }
}
```

The code defines a window that contains two labels and a panel, with the panel being
coloured yellow (this is achieved by means of the method `setBackground`, which uses
the static variable `Color.yellow`). When the mouse is clicked within the panel the
labels display the *x*- and *y*-coordinates of the point within the panel that the mouse was
clicked in. The methods `getX` and `getY` from the class `MouseEvent` are used to
retrieve these values from the `MouseEvent` argument. Figure 3 (overleaf) shows the
program working.

Figure 3   The frame **MouseFrame** showing the *x*- and *y*-coordinates of the point where the mouse was clicked in the lower panel

The class MouseFrame provides implementations for the five methods that are contained in MouseListener. However, since we are not reacting to four of the events, the code for the four corresponding methods is empty.

3.2 Adapters

Programming empty code for methods that cater for events we are not interested in is tedious, and a better solution is available in Java. The solution involves what are known as **adapter classes**. These are classes that are analogues of the interfaces, which implement the methods asked for by the interfaces by means of providing the empty code bodies. They allow the programmer who wants to react to a small number of events to inherit from these adapter classes. An example of an adapter class is MouseAdapter. This class provides empty bodies for the five methods detailed above.

We use adapters in the same way as listeners by defining inner classes, except now we extend rather than implement. This is because adapters are classes (albeit somewhat empty classes) rather than interfaces, unlike listeners. So the above code for class MouseFrame can be rewritten as:

```
import java.awt.*;
import java.awt.event.*;
import javax.swing.*;

public class NewMouser extends JFrame
{
    private JLabel yCoordLabel;
    private JLabel xCoordLabel;
    private JPanel c;
```

```
public NewMouser (String title)
{
    super(title);
    setSize(300, 300);
    yCoordLabel = new JLabel("");
    xCoordLabel = new JLabel("");
    c = new JPanel();
    c.setBackground(Color.yellow);
    getContentPane().setLayout(new GridLayout(3, 1));
    getContentPane().add(yCoordLabel);
    getContentPane().add(xCoordLabel);
    getContentPane().add(c);
    c.addMouseListener(new MouseEventer());
}


// inner class
private class MouseEventer extends MouseAdapter
{
    public void mouseClicked (MouseEvent e)
    {
        int xCoordinate = e.getX();
        int yCoordinate = e.getY();
        yCoordLabel.setText(yCoordinate + "");
        xCoordLabel.setText(xCoordinate + "");
    }
} // end of inner class
}
```

The inner class MouseEventer extends MouseAdapter. An instance of MouseEventer is created and registered as a listener within the constructor of the class NewMouser.

3.3 Window listeners

We are now in a position to tackle one of the irritating issues that we have had to deal with so far. That is, the fact that when any of the example programs are run, clicking on the close window icon does not end the program, it simply closes the window. Clicking the close window icon closes the window because that is the action of that icon, but it does not interact with any programs that we have written. We are now in a position to link the clicking of that icon with our program code. We will use the WindowAdapter class, which is the adapter class for the WindowListener interface and contains seven methods including windowOpening, windowClosing and windowClosed. We will use the windowClosing method to link the clicking of the close window icon with our program and get the program to stop when the window is closed.

As before, we will first define a class to close and quit the program:

```
import java.awt.event.*;

public class CloseAndQuit extends WindowAdapter
{
    public void windowClosing (WindowEvent e)
    {
        System.exit(0);
    }
}
```

We have defined `CloseAndQuit` by extending `WindowAdapter`. In this case, we have provided it as a stand-alone class, rather than as an inner class. This is partly to show that listeners can be stand-alone classes, but also because in this case `CloseAndQuit` does not need access to any of the variables and methods of the surrounding class and is not as logically connected to the main program. The class `CloseAndQuit` is a *general* class that we will be using in all of our visual programs from now onward and by defining it once we will be able to avoid including it in all of our code.

Having defined the listener class `CloseAndQuit`, we now add an instance of the class to the window using:

```
addWindowListener(new CloseAndQuit());
```

So long as the class `CloseAndQuit` is in the same package as the program we are running, then the above line of code will work.

As an example, we will take the program in the previous section – `NewMouser` – and add the above single line anywhere in the constructor (after the call to `super`, of course). By putting the class `CloseAndQuit` into the same package as `NewMouser` we will see that when we click the `close` icon on the window, the whole program stops.

Java provides its own equivalent to the `CloseAndQuit` class and it is a part of the `JFrame` class. Rather than defining your own class and adding the window listener in the constructor, you can simply include the following line in the constructor:

```
setDefaultCloseOperation(JFrame.EXIT_ON_CLOSE);
```

This method will set the operation that is to occur when the user initiates a 'close' on this frame. In this case the operation is to close the window and exit the program. You will see an example of using this method in Subsection 5.4.

3.4 Key listeners

In this section, we discuss how keyboard events are handled. As an example, we create a window with one text field, which has a listener to listen to events that are generated by keys. The listener is implemented by an inner class `KeyList`, which extends the adapter class `KeyAdapter`. This is the least troublesome solution to program since the `KeyListener` class contains more methods than those we require: `keyTyped`, `keyReleased` and the method that we will override in the inner class, `keyPressed`. This method is invoked whenever a key is pressed by the user. In our example, it checks whether the delete key has been pressed and then removes the text that is contained in the text field. The delete key is represented by the static constant `VK_DELETE`, which forms part of the `KeyEvent` class. Other static constants include `VK_ENTER` and `VK_TAB`. This example follows the pattern of all the others: the `KeyList` object constructed in the `KeyFrame` constructor is registered as a key event observer within the same constructor.

```java
import java.awt.*;
import java.awt.event.*;
import javax.swing.*;

public class KeyFrame extends JFrame
{
    private JTextField tf;

    public KeyFrame (String title)
    {
        super(title);
        setSize(300, 300);
        tf = new JTextField(20);
        getContentPane().setLayout(new FlowLayout());
        getContentPane().add(tf);
        tf.addKeyListener(new KeyList());

        // add CloseAndQuit
        addWindowListener(new CloseAndQuit());
    }

    // inner class
    private class KeyList extends KeyAdapter
    {
        public void keyPressed (KeyEvent k)
        {
            if (k.getKeyCode() == KeyEvent.VK_DELETE)
            {
                tf.setText("");
            }
        }
    }   // end of inner class
}   // end of KeyFrame

public class KeyFrameTest
{
    public static void main (String[] args)
    {
        KeyFrame world = new KeyFrame("KeyFrame");
        world.setVisible(true);
    }
}
```

3.5 Other listeners

The examples given in the previous sections will be sufficient to show you how to link any event to your program code, because the pattern is the same in *every* case. This is the power of the Swing system.

We have introduced you here to the basic approach to event programming. There are of course many more subtle issues that we could have looked at, such as defining classes that combine a component with its listener. For example, we can define a button that will listen for itself being clicked. In a program, we then simply create instances of these buttons as normal, but they have the added advantage of containing the necessary code to act on the event of their being clicked. In this case, we would define a button that extended `JButton` and implemented `ActionListener`. We will leave this as an activity for you to pursue when you have sufficient time available.

Other common listeners that you will encounter include:

▶ `AdjustmentListener`, which contains the single method `adjustmentValueChanged(AdjustmentEvent)` and is used by `JScrollBar`;

▶ `ItemListener`, which contains the single method `itemStateChanged` `(ItemEvent)` and is used by `JCheckBox` and `JComboBox`;

▶ `ListSelectionListener`, which is used by `JList` and contains the single method `valueChanged(ListSelectionEvent)`.

As we have done many times before, we urge you to use the Java reference facilities in your IDE to find out what is available. One of the advantages and disadvantages of Java is the existence of huge numbers of different libraries, and being aware of what is available is useful.

SAQ 3

(a) What events can be associated with a list component?

(b) Why did we need to define empty methods for the four methods that we didn't use in the `MouseWatcher` class?

(c) How do we know that an adapter, and not an interface, is being used in a class definition?

ANSWERS ....

(a) List components can be associated with action events, item events, component events and focus events.

(b) We need to define empty methods because listeners are interfaces (in the Java programming sense) and all methods have to be defined when the interface is implemented.

(c) We know an adapter has been used through the use of the `extends` keyword. If an interface had been used, the keyword would have been `implements`.

Activity 7.2
Constructing a window capable of knowing when the mouse is over it.

4 Graphics

Using the predefined Swing components is ideal for many graphical user interfaces. However, sometimes it is necessary to be able to create alternative images on screen. In these situations, we make use of **Graphics**.

4.1 Drawing methods

Many applications require drawing. For example, if you were developing an application that carried out the graphical display of data, say in a pie chart, then you would need to draw a circle and some lines and also fill in areas with some colour.

There is a special class known as `Graphics` that enables drawing to take place. The `Graphics` class is an abstract class that provides a graphical context for drawing, which the local Java system translates to the actual graphics device that is being used when the graphics operations occur.

The drawing process is achieved by means of the programmer providing a concrete implementation of a painting method, taking a `Graphics` object as its argument, and carrying out drawing actions on that object, which will be displayed on a screen. If you look in the Java class library you will find that the class `Component`, which forms the basis of all the GUI objects, has a `paint` method in it. Hence all the elements of the Swing toolkit inherit this method.

The `paint` method is invoked whenever a GUI object is created or some external action that requires redrawing (such as a window being moved) occurs. It is usually called indirectly by the program through such methods as `repaint` and `setVisible`. An example of the use of `paint` is shown below:

```java
import javax.swing.*;
import java.awt.Graphics;

public class SimpleGraphic extends JFrame
{
    /* Here we override the method paint to
    create what we want to appear on screen. */
    public void paint (Graphics g)
    {
        super.paint(g);
        g.drawRect(50, 50, 100, 75);
    }

    public SimpleGraphic (String title)
    {
        super(title);
        setSize(300, 300);
        addWindowListener(new CloseAndQuit());
    }
}
```

```
public class SimpleGraphicTest
{
    public static void main (String[] args)
    {
        SimpleGraphic world = new SimpleGraphic("Simple Graphic");
        world.setVisible(true);
    }
}
```

In this example, as shown in Figure 4, a rectangle is drawn at an offset (50, 50) from the origin, with a width of 100 and height of 75. The measurements are expressed in **pixels**, which stands for 'picture elements'. A picture element represents a single dot in a displayed image.

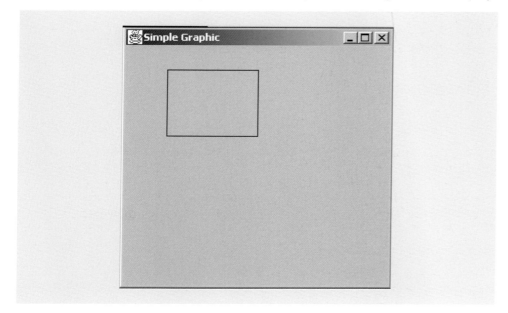

Figure 4   A **SimpleGraphic** frame showing a rectangle

We have shown the use of the `paint` method here for illustration, however in general it is recommended that you write your drawing code in a `paintComponent` method in a `JPanel` subclass (or another subclass of `JComponent`) and then add this component to your top-level container, such as a `JFrame` (or one of its subclasses), as shown in Unit 6 on pages 31 (`SwingClass3`) and 32 (`MyCanvas`).

The origin on an application is at the topmost left-hand position in the window. The x-direction then increases across the screen to the right and the y-direction increases down the screen. There are a number of methods available that allow us to draw closed figures and lines. A selection of these methods are described in Table 2.

Table 2 Methods to draw figures and lines

Method name	Description
drawRect(int,int,int,int)	This draws the outline of the specified rectangle using the current colour. The top left-hand corner of the rectangle is defined by a pair of x- and y-coordinates. The final two arguments give the *width* and *height*.
drawLine(int,int,int,int)	This draws a line, using the current colour, between the first pair of points and the second pair of points.

Table 2 *continued*

Method name	Description
drawRoundRect(int,int,int, int,int,int)	This draws the outline of a rectangle with rounded corners using the current colour. The top left-hand corner of the rectangle is defined by *x*- and *y*-coordinates, which are the first two arguments; the rectangle's *width* is the third argument and its *height* is the fourth argument. The final two arguments give the *width* and *height* of the arcs used to create the rounded corners.
drawOval(int,int,int,int)	This draws the outline of an oval. The result is a circle or an ellipse that fits within the rectangle whose top left-hand corner is specified by the first two arguments, whose *width* is given by the third argument and whose *height* is specified by the final argument.
drawString(String,int,int)	This draws the specified string using the current font and colour. The starting position of the string is defined by the *x*- and *y*-coordinates.
drawPolygon(Polygon)	This draws the outline of a polygon defined by the specified Polygon object.
fill3DRect(int,int,int,int, boolean)	This paints a filled 3D rectangle using the current colour. The first two arguments are the *x*- and *y*-coordinates of the top left-hand corner of the rectangle, the next two are the *width* and *height*, and the final argument indicates whether or not the rectangle is *raised* (it is, if the boolean argument evaluates to true).
fillArc(int,int,int,int, int, int)	This fills a sector using the current colour. The first two arguments are the *x* and *y* starting coordinates, the next two arguments are the *width* and *height* of the arc, the fifth argument is the starting angle of the arc and the last argument is the final angle. All angles are in degrees.
fillOval(int,int,int,int)	This fills an oval inside the specified rectangle using the current colour. The first two arguments give the coordinates of the left-hand corner of the bounding rectangle. The final two arguments give the *width* and *height* of the rectangle.
fillPolygon(int[],int[], int)	This fills a polygon with the current colour. The polygon's *x*-values are held in the first array and its *y*-values in the second array. The third argument represents the number of sides to the polygon.

The **Rectangle** class

In the drawPolygon method above, you will have noticed that the single argument was an instance of Polygon. Within the Java library, there are two classes that enable us to handle two-dimensional shapes efficiently. These are Rectangle, which deals with rectangles, and Polygon, which is more generalized and deals with any two-dimensional shape. The advantage of using these classes is that they not only hold all of the relevant bits of information about a shape but also contain useful methods for comparing and manipulating shapes.

We will illustrate this with a brief look at the Rectangle class.

There are many constructors for Rectangle using a variety of arguments. Some of the common ones are:

```
// top left at (0, 0) width 0, height 0
Rectangle r1 = new Rectangle();
// top left at (0, 0)
Rectangle r2 = new Rectangle(width, height);
// top left at (x, y)
Rectangle r3 = new Rectangle(x, y, width, height);
```

All of the above constructors have arguments that are integers. However, there are also constructors that use a Point argument. A Point is an object that can hold useful information (x- and y-values) and useful methods for manipulation. The simplest way to create a Point is:

```
Point p1 = new Point (20, 50);
```

After the above statement, p1 represents the point (20, 50). We can get access to the point's x- and y-coordinates using p1.x and p1.y respectively.

The constructor using the Point argument p1 can be invoked as follows:

```
Rectangle r4 = new Rectangle (p1);
```

This creates a rectangle with its top left-hand position at (20, 50) and both its width and height set to 0.

Table 3 shows some useful methods and fields of the Rectangle class.

Table 3 Methods and fields of **Rectangle** class

Method or field	Description
r1.equals (r2);	true if two rectangles are equal in terms of location and dimensions
r1.contains (x, y);	true if the point represented by the two arguments is inside the Rectangle r1
r1.intersects(r2);	true if the two rectangles r1 and r2 intersect
r1.add (x, y);	grows rectangle r1 to include (x, y)
r1.x, r1.y, r1.width, r1.height	the basic attributes of a rectangle

These are just a selection of the methods you can use for drawing. These and a number of other drawing methods can be found in the class java.awt.Graphics. Again, you will need to look at the Java reference material to see the full range of available methods.

Activity 7.3
Designing a logo.

4.2   Fonts and colour

The AWT also provides support for fonts and colours. The model adopted by Java to communicate colours to drawing methods and fonts to methods that display strings and characters is to set a *current* colour and a *current* font. This colour and font are used by all the `Graphics` methods until such time as they are reset to other values.

In Java, there are two classes that relate directly to font support: the `Font` class and the abstract `FontMetrics` class. The `Font` class is usually the most frequently used, while `FontMetrics` is required when information about an existing instance of `Font` is needed.

The `Font` class defines the font itself, including the font family, size and style. For example, to create a font in Serif, at 12 point and in bold you would use:

```
someFont = new Font("Serif", Font.BOLD, 12);
```

The first parameter to the constructor is a string that defines the font family. The next parameter is a static `int` variable from the `Font` class that defines the font as being bold. Finally, the last integer is the size of the type.

Once an instance of `Font` has been created, it can be used to define the appearance of text in a display. For example, in a `JPanel`, the following would be possible:

```
public void paintComponent(Graphics g)
{
    Font someFont = new Font("Serif", Font.BOLD, 12);
    g.setFont(someFont);
    g.drawString("Some Text!", 50, 50);
}
```

In this example, the `paintComponent` method defines a new font and then, by using the `setFont` method, instructs the `Graphics` context to set this as the font for further graphics operations. The next operation uses text and displays a string in the context. Because the font for the context was set prior to the call to `drawString` the text will be drawn using the font that was created.

The `FontMetrics` class can be used to obtain information about a particular font. This information is most useful when the display of an application requires the accurate positioning of components or when text needs to be formatted in a particular manner. The `FontMetrics` constructor requires an instance of `Font` as a parameter. For example:

```
Font aFont = new Font("Serif", Font.BOLD, 12);
Graphics g = this.getGraphics();
FontMetrics someFontMetric = g.getFontMetrics(aFont);
```

First of all, the `getGraphics` method obtains the graphics context for the application and having obtained this, the `getFontMetrics` method can be invoked. Once we have access to an instance of `FontMetrics`, it is possible to use the methods of that class to return information about the font. Some of the methods in the class include `stringWidth(String)` and `charWidth(char)`, which return the pixel widths of strings and characters in the font that was used to create the instance. For example, the code:

```
int wordLength = someFontmetric.stringWidth("Hello");
int charLength = someFontmetric.charWidth('h');
```

places in `wordLength` the width of the string `"Hello"` and in `charLength` the width of the character `'h'`.

As an example of using these methods, imagine that you require the title of a file to be centred in a window. If the filename is obtained from a text field, for example, there is no way of knowing the filename in advance and therefore it is impossible to know what the required offset is to ensure that the name of the file is centred as expected. However, by creating an instance of `FontMetric`, it is a simple matter to determine the width of the filename using `stringWidth` and then centre the string based on the width of the parent window. Other related methods return the height, ascent and descent of a font.

The `Color` class

The `Color` class (note the spelling) encapsulates **RGB colours**, where RGB stands for red, green and blue. The RGB values allow us to create a huge range of colours because all colours can be created from a combination of the three primary colours – red, green and blue. The RGB system allows you to define a particular colour by specifying either three integer values between 0 and 255 or three floating-point numbers in the range of 0.0 to 1.0. The value 255 is used simply to allow each value to be stored as an 8-bit byte. If we choose 0, 0, 0 (or 0.0, 0.0, 0.0) then the colour is black; if we choose 255, 255, 255 (or 1.0, 1.0, 1.0) then the colour is white. The colours are used to define the appearance of text, graphics primitives and graphical user interface components. To create a `Color`, there are several constructors that are supported, as shown in Table 4.

Table 4 Examples of constructors for `Color` class

`Color` constructor	Description
`Color(int,int,int)`	this creates a `Color` with each `int` representing a value (in the range 0 to 255) for the red, green and blue colours
`Color(int)`	this creates a `Color` with the bits of the integer representing values for the different colours (0 to 7 blue, 8 to 15 green and 16 to 23 red)
`Color(float,float,float)`	this creates a `Color` with each of red, green and blue colours being defined by a `float` in the range 0.0 to 1.0

So, for example, to create a colour where all three colours are set to 100, we can write the following statement:

```
Color myColor = new Color(100, 100, 100);
```

This results in `myColor` referring to some dark grey colour. However, most of the time there is no need to define colours with such precision and so the `Color` class defines a number of standard colours for general use. The range of colours is black, blue, cyan, darkGray, gray, green, lightGray, magenta, orange, pink, red, white and yellow. To use one of these predefined colours, for example green, use the following statement:

```
Color myColor = Color.green;
```

These predefined colours can be found in the class `java.awt.Color`. Once you have defined a colour, you can use it in your interface code. For example:

```
public void paintComponent (Graphics g)
{
    Color myColor = Color.green;
    g.setColor(myColor);
    g.fillRect(50, 50, 100, 100);
}
```

Once a colour has been set, any subsequent operations are performed using this colour. Consequently, it makes sense to group together the operations that require the same colours and fonts in your code in order to avoid switching more than you really need to.

When using colour in your interface, remember that Java colour support is not device-independent, and some colours will look different on a range of client machines.

4.3 Animation

Activity 7.4
Creating a coloured word game.

Now that you are able to produce images using lines, geometric shapes and colours, the natural next step is to look at producing images with the appearance of motion – that is, **animation**. The basic technique is to paint an image onto the screen and then paint a slightly different image onto the screen. If the changes between each image are sufficiently small and the repainting is done quickly enough, then the appearance of smooth motion can be achieved due to the 'persistence of vision' effect.

There are two main techniques for producing moving images. One approach, which we pursue here, is to generate each image as required. On a large scale this is computationally expensive but for the small images we use it is not a problem. This approach does have the advantage that the entire 'movie' is contained in the program code, which can then be sent to any Java-enabled device, such as a mobile phone. It also has the advantage of being able to react to user events that could not be anticipated beforehand.

The second approach to producing moving images is to have the individual images pre-prepared and then to load up each image and display it in turn. Each individual image could be a digitized 'real' image or have been generated by a computer (or some mixture of the two). This approach has the advantage that huge amounts of time can be spent on generating each image and all that is needed is the computing power to recall and display each image. This is the approach taken by the film industry and we will touch lightly on it.

We will look at a simple example that illustrates the potential of the first approach.

Moving ball

The class `MovingBall` and its associated class `Ball`, as shown below, create a very simple moving image (see Figure 5 on page 30). A red ball is created at some random point on the screen and it then falls at a constant speed down the screen. In the next section, we shall see how this can be developed into a simple game.

We have taken a prototyping approach of using the `paint` method in the `JFrame` rather than the more extensible approach of painting in a `JPanel` that is added to the `JFrame`.

```java
import java.awt.*;
import javax.swing.*;
import java.awt.event.*;

public class MovingBall extends JFrame
{
    protected final int FRAME_WIDTH = 240;
    protected final int FRAME_HEIGHT = 320;
    private Ball myBall = new Ball(FRAME_WIDTH, FRAME_HEIGHT);

    public MovingBall (String title)
    {
        super(title);
        setSize(FRAME_WIDTH, FRAME_HEIGHT);
        addWindowListener(new CloseAndQuit());
    }

    public void paint (Graphics g)
    {
        super.paint(g);
        myBall.paint(g);
    }

    public void move ()
    {
        while (true)
        {
            myBall.move();
            repaint();
            try
            {
                Thread.sleep(50);
            }
            catch (InterruptedException e)
            {
                System.exit(0);
            }
        }
    }
}

public class MovingBallTest
{
    public static void main (String[] args)
    {
        MovingBall world = new MovingBall("Moving Ball");
        world.setVisible(true);
        world.move();
    }
}
```

Figure 5   A **MovingBall** frame showing a ball

The class MovingBall sets up a frame of 240 by 320 pixels, which is a typical PDA-sized screen. It then repeatedly calls the method move, which in turn calls the method move of the class Ball that we shall look at shortly. After this, the method repaint is called. Note that we have not defined a method repaint, but it is inherited from Component. The repaint method calls the paint method, which we *have* defined but *cannot* call directly. This approach is part of the Java system to ensure that components are drawn in the correct order. In paint we tell the system *what* to paint; by calling repaint, we indicate that we wish this event to take place.

What is actually specified in the paint method is a call to super.paint(), which in effect clears the screen and redraws the background. You may wish to try taking out the call to super; you will see that the moving ball becomes a smear because the previous drawings of the ball are not being cleared. We then call the paint method of Ball.

In the move method, there is a try-catch block and the code Thread.sleep(50). The sleep method of the Thread class suspends the program for a period of time given in milliseconds. While the program sleeps, the system has time to finish the time-consuming process of repainting the window. You will learn more about the Thread class in a later unit. Again, try taking out the try-catch block. This time you will see that the ball is always at the bottom of the frame because the system has not had time to repaint the screen before the ball reaches the bottom.

On some systems there may be a flickering effect from the background frame. This arises because the whole frame is redrawn in the background colour each time the program loops, when repaint calls a method called update (also inherited from Component), which in turn calls paint. If the flickering occurs on your system (and only if it does) then by overriding update rather than paint you can avoid the flicker.

Essentially, we see that `MovingBall` sets up the scene, but all of the actual work is done by the `myBall` object. This object knows how to paint itself when asked and it also knows how to move.

```java
import java.awt.*;

public class Ball
{
    private final int RADIUS = 10;
    private Point pos;
    private Color ballColour = Color.red;
    private final int CHANGE = 3;
    private int height, width;

    public Ball (int frameWidth, int frameHeight)
    {
        width = frameWidth;
        height = frameHeight;
        pos = new Point ();
        pos.x = (int)(Math.random() * (width – RADIUS)) + RADIUS;
        pos.y = (int)(Math.random() * (height/2 – RADIUS)) + RADIUS;
    }

    public void paint (Graphics g)
    {
        g.setColor(ballColour);
        g.fillOval(pos.x – RADIUS, pos.y – RADIUS, 2 * RADIUS,
                    2 * RADIUS);
    }

    public void move ()
    {
        if (pos.y < height – RADIUS)
        {
            pos.translate(0, CHANGE);
        }
    }
}
```

Here we randomly create a starting position for the ball and define `paint`, which sets the colour and draws the ball itself. The method `move` contains the code that says what we mean by `move`. In this case, it is simply to go downwards by some amount until the bottom is reached. However, this code can be quite complex if you want the ball to bounce realistically. We have also used one of the other constructors of the `Point` class and the `translate` method from that class.

Although this is a simple example, by changing the code in `move` the ball can move in more complex ways, and by changing the code in `paint` the ball can become any shape you care to devise. You can even create many balls on screen at once with a simple loop in the `MovingBall` class. We shall see in a later unit how we can have many objects on screen, all moving independently of each other and even interacting with each other.

Images

We complete this section on animation with a brief study of the alternative approach to creating moving images on screen – that of displaying preformed images at a suitable speed. Java has a very rich collection of classes and methods to achieve this task. The main class is the `Image` class. For example:

```
private Image picture = null;
```

An image can then be assigned to variable `picture` from a file in GIF, JPEG or PNG format. Images can also be accessed using a URL:

```
picture = getToolKit().getImage("mypicture.gif");
```

This would assign the image `mypicture.gif` to variable `picture`. An image is then displayed using `drawImage` within a `paint` method:

```
g.drawImage(picture, 0, 0, this);
```

There are several `drawImage` methods in the `Graphics` class. The above example takes as its arguments an `Image`, the x- and y-coordinates to draw at and an `ImageObserver`. In this case, the `ImageObserver` is the main class itself and it is simply acting as somewhere to receive notifications about `Image` information as the `Image` is constructed. This is denoted by the use of the Java keyword `this`.

Using these basic classes and methods, typically many images would be loaded into an array or vector. These would then be displayed with a suitable 'sleep' period to allow the images to be drawn and to fool the eye into seeing a moving image rather than a slide show of individual images. Look in the Java reference documentation under `Image` class and `Graphics` class for more details.

SAQ 4

(a) What line of code creates a circle with a radius of 10 pixels centred at position (100, 100)?

(b) Write a short piece of code that creates a `Point` object referenced by `poin` at location (100, 100). Use this to create a `Rectangle` object called `rect` with top left-hand corner at (100, 100) with a height and width of 0. Then expand `rect` to include the location (200, 200).

(c) In the `paint` method of `MovingBall` we call `super.paint(g)`. Why don't we do the same in the `paint` method of `Ball`?

ANSWERS ....

(a) `g.drawOval(90, 90, 20, 20);` note that (90, 90) is the location of the top left-hand corner of a box of width 20 and height 20.

(b) The three statements are as follows:

```
Point poin = new Point(100, 100);
Rectangle rect = new Rectangle(poin);
rect.add(200, 200);
```

(c) In `MovingBall` the `paint` method is producing the whole picture, which includes the frame and the current image of the ball. So we get the frame painted by calling the parent (`JFrame`) of `MovingBall` to paint itself. In `Ball`, the `paint` method has only to paint its current self.

Activity 7.5
Experimenting with animation.

5 Some examples

We conclude this unit with the following four examples. Each of these covers the techniques that we have described in the previous sections. The examples also flesh out some of the points that we may have skated over in the earlier sections.

5.1 Mouse clicker

The first example displays a panel. When the user clicks at a point in the panel a message is displayed. The user can switch the colour in which the message is displayed by clicking a radio button. In Figure 6, we see the radio buttons (the blue button has been clicked) and the result of a number of clicks on the panel in the top half of the screen. The text displayed is the string 'Hello there'.

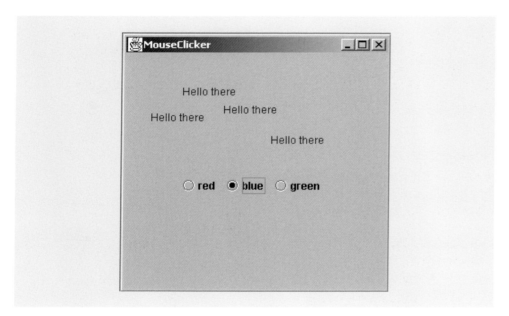

Figure 6   The **MouseClicker** frame showing the text **Hello there** in the chosen colour in a variety of positions on the screen

The main class for this application is shown below:

```
public class MouseClickerTest
{
    public static void main (String[] args)
    {
        MouseClicker world = new MouseClicker();
        world.setVisible(true);
    }
}
```

```java
// the MouseClicker class
import java.awt.*;
import javax.swing.*;
import java.awt.event.*;

public class MouseClicker extends JFrame
{
    private Color currentColour;
    private JRadioButton redButton;
    private JRadioButton blueButton;
    private JRadioButton greenButton;
    private JPanel bottom;
    private ClickablePanel top;

    public MouseClicker()
    {
        setTitle("MouseClicker");
        setSize(300, 300);
        ButtonGroup colour = new ButtonGroup();
        bottom = new JPanel();
        top = new ClickablePanel();
        redButton = new JRadioButton("red", true);
        bottom.add(redButton);
        blueButton = new JRadioButton("blue", false);
        bottom.add(blueButton);
        greenButton = new JRadioButton("green", false);
        bottom.add(greenButton);

        // now add the radio buttons to the button group
        colour.add(redButton);
        colour.add(blueButton);
        colour.add(greenButton);

        getContentPane().setLayout(new GridLayout(2, 1));
        getContentPane().add(top);
        getContentPane().add(bottom);

        redButton.addItemListener(new ButtonWatcher());
        blueButton.addItemListener(new ButtonWatcher());
        greenButton.addItemListener(new ButtonWatcher());
        addWindowListener(new CloseAndQuit());
    } // ends constructor
}
```

In MouseClicker we have declared two panel variables, one a JPanel and the other a ClickablePanel, which we will define later. We have created a radio button group and attached an ItemListener to each button. This ItemListener is defined below as an inner class. The radio buttons have been placed on the bottom panel and both panels have been added to the frame. The code also declares currentColour, which will reference the current colour in which text is displayed on the panel.

The next code segment is that for handling the event of a radio button being checked. The code is shown below:

```
private class ButtonWatcher implements ItemListener
{
    public void itemStateChanged (ItemEvent i)
    {
        if (redButton.isSelected())
        {
            currentColour = Color.red;
        }
        if (blueButton.isSelected())
        {
            currentColour = Color.blue;
        }
        if (greenButton.isSelected())
        {
            currentColour = Color.green;
        }
        top.setClickColour(currentColour);
    } // ends method itemStateChanged
} // ends class ButtonWatcher
```

The `ItemListener` interface has a method `itemStateChanged`, and here we have provided the implementation for it. Since the constructor has added an instance of `ButtonWatcher` to each of the radio buttons, this code is executed when any of these buttons is clicked. The method `isSelected` returns `true` if the radio button is in the 'on' position (for example, the blue button in Figure 6).

All that is now needed is to program the `ClickablePanel` class. The first lines of this class are shown below:

```
import java.awt.*;
import javax.swing.*;
import java.awt.event.*;

public class ClickablePanel extends JPanel
{
    private int[] xVals,yVals;
    private int numberOfClicks;
    private Color colour;
    private Clicker cl;
```

This class inherits from `JPanel`. It contains instance variables that hold the current colour used for writing the strings, the number of clicks that have occurred within this component, and two arrays that hold the *x*- and *y*-values of each click that has occurred. It also holds an instance variable for the instance of the inner class `Clicker`, which is used to track mouse clicks.

The constructor of the `ClickablePanel` class is shown below. It sets up the panel, initializes the number of clicks, sets the first colour to red (`Color.red`) and allocates memory for the arrays. It also registers the instance variable `cl` as a mouse listener, which is a very important statement. It is this line of code that turns an ordinary panel into a clickable panel because it now has the capability to listen to mouse clicks.

Note that when `redButton` is created in the `MouseClicker` constructor, it has `true` as one of its arguments, unlike the other buttons. This shows that it is up to the application programmer to ensure that the look of the button corresponds to what is set as the default colour. This button is selected when the GUI is first displayed.

```
public ClickablePanel()
{
    super();
    cl = new Clicker();
    addMouseListener(cl);
    colour = Color.red;
    xVals = new int[100];
    yVals = new int[100];
    numberOfClicks = 0;
}
```

Two further methods of the ClickablePanel class are shown below:

```
public void setClickColour (Color c)
{
    colour = c;
}


public void paintComponent (Graphics g)
{
    super.paintComponent(g);
    g.setColor(colour);
    for (int i = 0; i < numberOfClicks; i++)
    {
        g.drawString("Hello there", xVals[i], yVals[i]);
    }
}
```

The first method, setClickColour, is used in the ButtonWatcher class and simply sets the current colour. The next method overrides the default paintComponent method supplied with the JPanel class. This method is the JPanel analogue of the paint method of JFrame. The paintComponent method sets the colour for drawing to the current colour and then draws all the instances of the string "Hello there" on the panel. The code uses the methods drawString and setColor provided as part of the Color class in the java.awt package.

The inner class is shown below:

```
    private class Clicker extends MouseAdapter
    {
        public void mouseClicked (MouseEvent m)
        {
            xVals[numberOfClicks] = m.getX();
            yVals[numberOfClicks] = m.getY();
            numberOfClicks++;
            repaint();
        }
    } // ends inner class Clicker
} // ends class ClickablePanel
```

This, then, is the code for our application. The code for ClickablePanel keeps track of the past mouse clicks and refreshes the screen with all the text that needs to be displayed. It does this by calling paintComponent via the repaint method when a relevant event occurs.

An important point to make about the code above is that some of it is vestigial but it has been placed there in order to clarify the mechanisms that are involved in using inner classes.

5.2 Colour selector

The second example demonstrates the use of some of the control elements we discussed in the earlier part of this unit. It uses three sliders to adjust the red, green and blue components of a colour and displays the resulting colour. Four panels are used: one displays the current red colour, another the current blue colour, another the current green colour and the final canvas displays the colour made by combining the red, green and blue components.

The display for this application is shown in Figure 7.

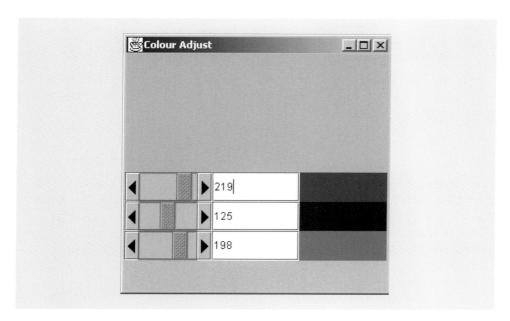

Figure 7   The **ColourAdjust** frame with the top panel showing the combination of the three colours selected using the sliders below

The topmost panel contains the mixed colour; below this are the three sliders with their respective values and colours. The first lines of the application are shown below:

```
public class ColourAdjustTest
{
    public static void main (String[] args)
    {
        ColourAdjust world = new ColourAdjust();
        world.setVisible(true);
    }
}
```

```java
import java.awt.*;
import javax.swing.*;
import java.awt.event.*;
public class ColourAdjust extends JFrame
{
    private JPanel bottom;
    private int greenValue;
    private int redValue;
    private int blueValue;
    private ColourPanel greenCanvas;
    private ColourPanel redCanvas;
    private ColourPanel blueCanvas;
    private ColourPanel colCanvas;
    private JTextField greenText;
    private JTextField blueText;
    private JTextField redText;
    private JScrollBar redSlider;
    private JScrollBar blueSlider;
    private JScrollBar greenSlider;
```

This declares the various sliders, text fields and panels necessary for the operation. The integer variables, greenValue, redValue and blueValue, are the colour values that are used to construct the composite colour.

```java
    public ColourAdjust ()
    {
        setTitle("Colour Adjust");
        setSize(300, 300);
        bottom = new JPanel();
        colCanvas = new ColourPanel();
        redCanvas = new ColourPanel();
        blueCanvas = new ColourPanel();
        greenCanvas = new ColourPanel();
        bottom.setLayout(new GridLayout(4, 3));
        redSlider = new JScrollBar(JScrollBar.HORIZONTAL, 0, 1, 0, 256);
        blueSlider = new JScrollBar(JScrollBar.HORIZONTAL, 0, 1, 0, 256);
        greenSlider = new JScrollBar(JScrollBar.HORIZONTAL, 0, 1, 0, 256);

        redText = new JTextField("0000", 4);
        blueText = new JTextField("0000", 4);
        greenText = new JTextField("0000", 4);

        bottom.add(redSlider);
        bottom.add(redText);
        bottom.add(redCanvas);
        bottom.add(blueSlider);
        bottom.add(blueText);
        bottom.add(blueCanvas);
        bottom.add(greenSlider);
        bottom.add(greenText);
        bottom.add(greenCanvas);
        getContentPane().setLayout(new GridLayout(2, 1));
        getContentPane().add(colCanvas);
        getContentPane().add(bottom);
        redSlider.addAdjustmentListener(new ColSlide());
        greenSlider.addAdjustmentListener(new ColSlide());
        blueSlider.addAdjustmentListener(new ColSlide());
    }
```

The code that handles a slider being modified is shown below. Again, we have used an inner class. It involves overriding the method `adjustmentValueChanged` of the interface `AdjustmentListener`. The method `getAdjustable` returns the slider that has changed.

```java
public class ColSlide implements AdjustmentListener
{
    public void adjustmentValueChanged (AdjustmentEvent e)
    {
        if ((e.getAdjustable()) == redSlider)
        {
            redValue = redSlider.getValue();
            redText.setText("" + redValue);
            redCanvas.changeColour(redValue, 0, 0);
            redCanvas.repaint();
        }
        if ((e.getAdjustable()) == blueSlider)
        {
            blueValue = blueSlider.getValue();
            blueText.setText("" + blueValue);
            blueCanvas.changeColour(0, 0, blueValue);
            blueCanvas.repaint();
        }
        if ((e.getAdjustable()) == greenSlider)
        {
            greenValue = greenSlider.getValue();
            greenText.setText("" + greenValue);
            greenCanvas.changeColour(0, greenValue, 0);
            greenCanvas.repaint();
        }
        colCanvas.changeColour(redValue, greenValue, blueValue);
        colCanvas.repaint();
    } // ends adjustmentValueChanged
    } // ends inner class ColSlide
} // ends ColourAdjust
```

The class defining a `ColourPanel` object is shown below:

```java
import java.awt.Graphics;
import javax.swing.*;
import java.awt.*;

public class ColourPanel extends JPanel
{
    private Color currColour;

    public Color getColour ()
    {
        return currColour;
    }
```

```
public void changeColour (int r, int g, int b)
{
    currColour = new Color (r, g, b);
}

public void paintComponent (Graphics g)
{
    Dimension d = getSize ();
    g.setColor(currColour);
    g.fillRect(0, 0, d.width, d.height);
}

public ColourPanel()
{
    currColour = new Color(0, 0, 0);
}
}
```

Activity 7.6
Running the
ColourAdjust **program.**

There are two things to note. First, it uses the constructor of `Color` that takes three integer values representing the red, green and blue components of a colour. Second, the `paintComponent` method associated with `ColourPanel` objects finds the size of the panel by applying the `getSize` method that is associated with the `Component` class. This method delivers a `Dimension` object that has two public instance variables, `width` and `height`. These are used to draw a filled rectangle on a panel using the current colour of the canvas.

5.3 CAD package

The next example is of an application that carries out the drawing of many-sided figures using a preselected colour and a preselected style so that the figure can either be an outline or be filled in. The user can draw many polygons in a variety of colours and styles on the same 'canvas'.

An example display for this application is shown in Figure 8.

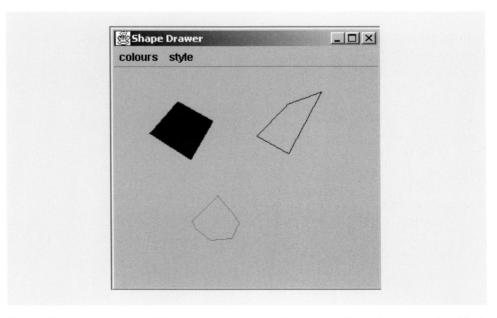

Figure 8   An example of **ShapeDrawer** showing two outline shapes and a filled shape

Colour and style are selected using drop-down menus. A panel is used to draw
n-sided figures using a mouse. The first time the user clicks the mouse determines the
starting location of the first side of the polygon. Any subsequent clicks will determine the
lengths of the other sides.

When the mouse clicks on the first position of the polygon again, the polygon is
complete and the current colour and style are applied to it. The first lines of the
application are shown below:

```
import javax.swing.*;
import java.awt.event.*;
import java.awt.*;

public class ShapeDrawer extends JFrame
{
    private final int FRAME_HEIGHT = 300;
    private final int FRAME_WIDTH = 300;
    private final String[] colourChoices = {"red", "blue", "green"};
    private final Color[] colChoices =
        {Color.red, Color.blue, Color.green};
    private final String[] drawChoices = { "outline", "filled"};
    private JMenuBar bar;
    private JMenu colours;
    private JMenu style;
    private JMenuItem[] col = new JMenuItem[colourChoices.length];
    private JMenuItem[] sty = new JMenuItem[drawChoices.length];
    private Color defaultcol = Color.red;
    private String defaultsty = "filled";
    private PaintCanvas canvas;
```

The above code sets up a `PaintCanvas` object (which is defined later) and a
`JMenuBar` with two sets of drop-down menu items.

Below is the constructor that puts all of the pieces together. The `JMenuItems` are given
their values, added to the `JMenus` and then set in a `JMenuBar`, which is added to the
frame along with the `PaintCanvas`.

```
    public ShapeDrawer (String title)
    {
        super(title);
        setSize(FRAME_WIDTH, FRAME_HEIGHT);
        bar = new JMenuBar();
        setJMenuBar(bar);
        canvas = new PaintCanvas(defaultcol, defaultsty);
        getContentPane().add(canvas);
        colours = new JMenu("colours");
        for (int i=0; i < colourChoices.length; i++)
        {
            col[i] = new JMenuItem(colourChoices[i]);
            col[i].addActionListener(new MenuSelection());
            colours.add(col[i]);
        }
        style = new JMenu("style");
```

```
    for (int i=0; i < drawChoices.length; i++)
    {
        sty[i] = new JMenuItem(drawChoices[i]);
        sty[i].addActionListener(new MenuSelection());
        style.add(sty[i]);
    }
    bar.add(colours);
    bar.add(style);
    addWindowListener(new CloseAndQuit());
}
```

We have now created the graphical user interface but, of course, nothing happens when you make a selection from the menus. Below is an inner class that listens for menu items being selected and then uses the choices to set the colour and the style of the drawing in the PaintCanvas object.

```
private class MenuSelection implements ActionListener
{
    public void actionPerformed (ActionEvent e)
    {
        for (int i = 0; i < colourChoices.length; i++)
        {
            if (e.getSource() == col[i])
            {
                canvas.setColour(colChoices[i]);
            }
        }
        for (int i = 0; i < drawChoices.length; i++)
        {
            if (e.getSource() == sty[i])
            {
                canvas.setStyle(drawChoices[i]);
            }
        } // ends for
    } // ends method actionPerformed
} // ends inner class MenuSelection
} // ends class ShapeDrawer
```

This ends the ShapeDrawer class. Note that the ShapeDrawer class makes use of a class called PaintCanvas that does all of the drawing work. The class extends JPanel and has a number of arrays that store the colours, styles and x- and y-coordinates (that define the shape and size of each polygon) for up to 100 polygons.

Each polygon can have up to 50 (*x*, *y*) coordinate pairs, which we will refer to as points, even though the `Point` class is not used in this example.

```java
import javax.swing.*;
import java.awt.event.*;
import java.awt.*;

public class PaintCanvas extends JPanel
{
    private Clicker cc;
    private Color[] polyColours;
    private String[] polyStyle;
    private Polygon[] polyStore;
    private int numberOfPoints;
    private int polyCount;
    private Color currentColour;
    private int[] yPoints;
    private int[] xPoints;
    private String currentStyle;

    public PaintCanvas (Color c, String sty)
    {
        super();
        currentColour = c;
        currentStyle = sty;
        polyCount = 0;
        numberOfPoints = 0;
        polyColours = new Color[100];
        polyStyle = new String[100];
        polyStore = new Polygon[100];
        xPoints = new int[50];
        yPoints = new int[50];
        cc = new Clicker(this);
        addMouseListener(cc);
    }
```

The mouse is used to indicate where the points of each polygon are located. The class `PaintCanvas` has an inner class, `Clicker`, which records the coordinates of each click and repaints the panel when there is more than one point. If a point comes close enough to the first point, it is assumed that the user intended that to be the end of the polygon. This allows for the user not being able to click *precisely* on the original spot. How close exactly is decided by the method `isCloseEnough` (belonging to class `PaintCanvas`), which uses Pythagoras' theorem to see whether the current point and the first point are within an arbitrary 10 pixels of each other. If they are, then the arrays holding the *x*- and *y*-coordinates are used to create a new `Polygon`, which is stored in an array of polygons.

```
private class Clicker extends MouseAdapter
{
    private PaintCanvas tpc;

    public Clicker (PaintCanvas pc)
    {
        tpc = pc;
    }
    public void mouseClicked (MouseEvent e)
    {
        int xVal = e.getX(), yVal = e.getY();
        xPoints[numberOfPoints] = xVal;
        yPoints[numberOfPoints] = yVal;
        numberOfPoints++;
        if (numberOfPoints > 1)
        {
            tpc.repaint();
        }
        if (numberOfPoints > 2 && isCloseEnough())
        {
            polyStore[polyCount] = new
                Polygon(xPoints, yPoints, numberOfPoints);
            polyColours[polyCount] = currentColour;
            polyStyle[polyCount] = currentStyle;
            polyCount++;
            numberOfPoints = 0;
            tpc.repaint();
        } // ends if
    } // ends method mouseClicked
} // ends inner class Clicker
```

The code for methods isCloseEnough, setColour and setStyle are given below. The isCloseEnough method uses the methods pow and sqrt, which are static methods in the Math class in the java.lang library. The pow method takes two arguments, the first a double value that is raised to the power indicated by the second (for squaring this is 2.0). The sqrt method returns the square root of its argument's value. Notice the use of the (double) cast, which makes sure that the integer values within the arrays holding the polygon points are of the right type for these two methods.

```
public boolean isCloseEnough ()
{
    double xLength = (double)(xPoints[0] − xPoints[numberOfPoints − 1]);
    double yLength = (double)(yPoints[0] − yPoints[numberOfPoints − 1]);
    double hypot = Math.sqrt(Math.pow(xLength, 2.0) +
                            Math.pow(yLength, 2.0));
    if (hypot < 10)
    {
        return true;
    }
    else
    {
        return false;
    }
}
```

```
public void setColour (Color c)
{
    currentColour = c;
}
public void setStyle (String s)
{
    currentStyle = s;
}
```

The final method of `PaintCanvas` class we now discuss is `paintComponent`. This method is called whenever the program calls `repaint`. In a sense, the program is inefficient in that it redraws everything every time. The first `for` loop draws the completed polygons in either the filled or the outline style. The second `for` loop draws the current polygon as it is being created by the user.

```
public void paintComponent (Graphics g)
{
    super.paintComponent(g);
    for (int i = 0; i < polyCount; i++)
    {
        g.setColor(polyColours[i]);
        if (polyStyle[i].equals("filled"))
        {
            g.fillPolygon(polyStore[i]);
        }
        else
        {
            g.drawPolygon(polyStore[i]);
        }
    }
    g.setColor(currentColour);
    for (int j = 0; j < numberOfPoints - 1; j++)
    {
        g.drawLine(xPoints[j], yPoints[j], xPoints[j + 1],
            yPoints[j + 1]);
    }
} // ends method paintComponent
) // ends class PaintCanvas
```

The method `isCloseEnough` in class `PaintCanvas` makes use of Pythagoras' theorem to see whether the current point and the first point are within an arbitrary 10 pixels of each other. However, the code for `isCloseEnough` is quite dense and so to help you follow it we will now give an example to draw out the mathematics.

Example using `isCloseEnough`

We will determine whether the two points (5, 5) and (12, 14) are within 10 pixels of each other and thus close enough to be considered the same. We will assume that (5, 5) is the starting point of the polygon, and that (12, 14) is the most recently clicked point.

If (5, 5) is the starting point then:

`xPoints[0] = 5`

`yPoints[0] = 5`

and with (12, 14) as the most recently clicked point then:

`xPoints[numberOfPoints - 1] = 12`

`yPoints[numberOfPoints - 1] = 14`

The rest of the calculations are as follows:

```
xLength = (double) 5 - 12
        = -7.0
yLength = (double) 5 - 14
        = -9.0
hypot   = Math.sqrt (Math.pow (-7.0, 2.0) + Math.pow (-9.0, 2.0))
        = Math.sqrt (49.0 + 81.0)
        = Math.sqrt (130.0)
        = 11.401
```

Hence the points (5, 5) and (12, 14) are more than 10 pixels apart and `isCloseEnough` will return `false`.

5.4   A ball game

The final example pulls together some of the ideas that we have met so far in this unit to create a simple ball game. It involves the user using the left and right arrow keys to move a 'paddle' in order to hit a moving ball. When the player hits the moving ball, then it bounces off and hits the sides of the box until it comes down again. The object of the game is to keep the ball 'up'. There is no scoring mechanism and the user has to run the program again to get another go. However, it includes almost all of the key elements of a game. The operation of the game is a little 'jerky' because the computer is checking for user input and moving the ball at the 'same time'. In *Unit 8* we will see a much more sophisticated way of getting the computer to do 'more than one thing at a time'.

The complete code for the various classes is given below. Some of the classes have been changed slightly. We will alert you to these changes and explain them when they occur.

The first class, `BallGame`, is a subclass of `MovingBall`, although the version of `MovingBall` that we are using is slightly different from the one we used before in Subsection 4.3. The class `BallGame` essentially deals with the user interaction using the `KeyAdapter` and checks to see whether the ball and the paddle, as shown in Figure 9, are sufficiently close to cause the ball to bounce.

Figure 9   The **BallGame** frame showing the ball and paddle

```
public class BallGameTest
{
    public static void main (String[] args)
    {
        BallGame world = new BallGame("Ball game");
        world.setVisible(true);
        world.move();
    }
}

import java.awt.Graphics;
import java.awt.event.*;

public class BallGame extends MovingBall
{
    private Paddle myPaddle = new Paddle(FRAME_WIDTH, FRAME_HEIGHT);

    public BallGame (String title)
    {
        super(title);
        addKeyListener(new KeyList());
    }
```

```
public void paint (Graphics g)
{
    super.paint(g);
    if (isContact())
    {
        myBall.bounce();
    }
    else
    {
        myPaddle.paint(g);
    }
}

public boolean isContact()
{
    if (myPaddle.area().contains(myBall.getPosition()))
    {
        return true;
    }
    else
    {
        return false;
    }
}

// inner class for the listener
private class KeyList extends KeyAdapter
{
    public void keyPressed (KeyEvent k)
    {
        if (k.getKeyCode() == KeyEvent.VK_LEFT)
        {
            myPaddle.moveLeft();
        }
        if (k.getKeyCode() == KeyEvent.VK_RIGHT)
        {
            myPaddle.moveRight();
        }
    } // ends method keyPressed
} // ends private class KeyList
} // ends class BallGame
```

In this version of MovingBall, some of the private fields have been changed to
protected in order to allow subclasses to be created. Furthermore, instead of using
CloseAndQuit, we illustrate the use of the setDefaultCloseOperation(JFrame.
EXIT_ON_CLOSE) statement.

```java
import java.awt.*;
import javax.swing.*;
import java.awt.event.*;

public class MovingBall extends JFrame
{
    protected final int FRAME_WIDTH = 240;
    protected final int FRAME_HEIGHT = 320;
    protected Ball myBall = new Ball(FRAME_WIDTH, FRAME_HEIGHT);

    public MovingBall (String title)
    {
        super(title);
        setSize(FRAME_WIDTH, FRAME_HEIGHT);
        setDefaultCloseOperation(JFrame.EXIT_ON_CLOSE);
    }

    public void paint (Graphics g)
    {
        super.paint(g);
        myBall.paint(g);
    }

    public void move ()
    {
        while (true)
        {
            myBall.move();
            repaint();
            try
            {
                Thread.sleep(50);
            }
            catch (InterruptedException e)
            {
                System.exit(0);
            }
        } // ends while
    } // ends move
} // ends MovingBall
```

Below is the `Ball` class. The main changes to `Ball` (compared to the version we studied in Subsection 4.3) are those to the `move` method and in the introduction of a new method, `bounce`. These methods cause the ball to 'bounce' off the sides of the frame as well as off the paddle if this is in the right place at the right time. A more sophisticated system could incorporate some 'noise' into the bounce, for example, but here we have implemented a simple version.

```java
import java.awt.*;

public class Ball
{
    private final int RADIUS = 10;
    private Point pos;
    private Color ballColour = Color.red;
    private int yChange = 2;
    private int xChange = 1;
    private int height, width;

    public Ball (int frameWidth, int frameHeight)
    {
        width = frameWidth;
        height = frameHeight;
        pos = new Point ();
        pos.x = (int)(Math.random() * (width - RADIUS)) + RADIUS;
        pos.y = (int)(Math.random() * (height/2 - RADIUS)) + RADIUS;
    }

    public void paint (Graphics g)
    {
        g.setColor(ballColour);
        g.fillOval(pos.x - RADIUS, pos.y - RADIUS, 2 * RADIUS, 2 * RADIUS);
    }

    public void move ()
    {
        if (pos.y < RADIUS)
        {
            yChange = -yChange;
        }
        if (pos.x < RADIUS)
        {
            xChange = -xChange;
        }
        if (pos.x > width - RADIUS)
        {
            xChange = -xChange;
        }
        if (pos.y < height - RADIUS)
        {
            pos.translate(xChange, yChange);
        }
        if (pos.x < width - RADIUS)
        {
            pos.translate(xChange, yChange);
        }
    }

    public void bounce ()
    {
        yChange = -yChange;
        pos.translate(xChange, yChange);
    }
```

```
    public Point getPosition ()
    {
        return pos;
    }
}
```

The final class is `Paddle`. This acts as the 'paddle' that the user moves along the bottom of the frame. As well as knowing how to paint itself and how to move to the left or to the right, it has a method called `area` that helps it to 'know its own extent'. The method `area` works by creating a `Rectangle` at the current position of the paddle. This `Rectangle` object is then used in the class `BallGame`, which is in the method `isContact`, to decide whether the ball and the paddle are in the same space and whether the ball should be instructed to bounce.

```
import java.awt.*;
import java.awt.event.*;
import javax.swing.*;

public class Paddle
{
    private Color paddleColour = Color.blue;
    private int x, y;
    private int paddleWidth = 20;
    private int paddleHeight = 10;
    private int move = 5;

    public Paddle (int frameWidth,int frameHeight)
    {
        x = (int)(Math.random() * (frameWidth - paddleWidth));
        y = frameHeight - paddleHeight;
    }

    public void moveRight ()
    {
        x = x + move;
    }

    public void moveLeft ()
    {
        x = x - move;
    }

    public Rectangle area ()
    {
        return new Rectangle(x, y, paddleWidth, paddleHeight);
    }

    public void paint (Graphics g)
    {
        g.setColor(paddleColour);
        g.fillRect(x, y, paddleWidth, paddleHeight);
    }
}
```

Activity 7.7
Creating 'framelets' –
editable notepads.

6 Summary

In this unit we have looked at the Java Event Model and described how you can use it to provide the link between a component on the screen, such as a button, and the code that you wish to execute when that button is clicked. This has involved the use of listeners and adapters and inner classes. We have also looked at simple animation and the graphical capabilities of Java. Section 5 describes four extended examples to illustrate how all of these elements work together. What we have shown you in the last two units are small samples of the classes and methods available in the Java API. In fact, the `swing` package alone contains something like 250 classes. It is therefore again worth stressing that the only way to program in Java is to have the API documentation next to you.

LEARNING OUTCOMES

When you have completed this unit, you should be able to:

▶ work within an event-driven programming environment;

▶ attach code to visual components to capture user input in the form of events such as mouse presses and text input;

▶ use inner classes;

▶ create simple animations;

▶ use the graphical facilities within Java.

Concepts

The following concepts have been introduced in this unit:

adapter, animation, event, event-driven programming, event source, `Graphics`, inner class, listener, pixel, `Polygon`, `Rectangle`, RGB colours.

Appendix 2 – calculator code

What follows is the complete code for the calculator GUI developed in *Unit 6*.

```java
public class RunningExampleTest
{
    public static void main (String[] args)
    {
        Calculator fd = new Calculator("Calculator Example");
        fd.setVisible(true);
    }
}


import java.awt.*;
import javax.swing.*;
import java.awt.event.*;

public class Calculator extends JFrame
{
    private final int NUMBER_KEY_PAD_BUTTONS = 10;
    private final int NUMBER_DIGITS = 25;
    private JButton[] keyPadButtons;
    private JButton clearButton;
    private JButton pointButton;
    private JPanel keyPadPanel;
    private JPanel displayPanel;
    private JPanel functionPanel;
    private JButton addButton;
    private JButton subtractButton;
    private JButton multiplyButton;
    private JButton divideButton;
    private JButton equalsButton;
    private JTextField displayField;
    private String currentDisplay;
    private String operand1;
    private int function;
    private double result;

    public Calculator (String title)
    {
        setSize(300, 300);
        setTitle(title);
        currentDisplay = "";

        /* Set up key pad panel containing number, CE and
        point buttons. */
        keyPadPanel = new JPanel();
        keyPadPanel.setLayout(new GridLayout(3, 4));
        keyPadButtons = new JButton[NUMBER_KEY_PAD_BUTTONS];
```

```
/* Create each number button, add to panel and add
action listener. */
for (int i = 0; i < NUMBER_KEY_PAD_BUTTONS; i++)
{
    keyPadButtons[i] = new JButton("" + i);
    keyPadPanel.add(keyPadButtons[i]);
    keyPadButtons[i].addActionListener(new
        KeyPadButtonWatcher());
}

/* Create CE and point button, add to panel and add
action listener. */
clearButton = new JButton("CE");
pointButton = new JButton(".");
keyPadPanel.add(clearButton);
keyPadPanel.add(pointButton);
clearButton.addActionListener(new KeyPadButtonWatcher());
pointButton.addActionListener(new KeyPadButtonWatcher());

// set up display field panel
displayPanel = new JPanel();
displayField = new JTextField(NUMBER_DIGITS);
displayField.setText("0.0");
displayPanel.add(displayField);

// create function panel and function buttons
functionPanel = new JPanel();
functionPanel.setLayout(new GridLayout(5, 1));
addButton = new JButton("+");
subtractButton = new JButton("-");
multiplyButton = new JButton("*");
divideButton = new JButton("/");
equalsButton = new JButton("=");

// add function buttons to panel
functionPanel.add(addButton);
functionPanel.add(subtractButton);
functionPanel.add(multiplyButton);
functionPanel.add(divideButton);
functionPanel.add(equalsButton);

// add action listeners to function buttons
addButton.addActionListener(new FunctionButtonWatcher());
subtractButton.addActionListener(new FunctionButtonWatcher());
multiplyButton.addActionListener(new FunctionButtonWatcher());
divideButton.addActionListener(new FunctionButtonWatcher());
equalsButton.addActionListener(new EqualsButtonWatcher());

// add functionality to close icon
setDefaultCloseOperation(JFrame.EXIT_ON_CLOSE);
```

```java
        // get content pane and add panels to frame
        Container cp = getContentPane();
        cp.add(displayPanel, BorderLayout.NORTH);
        cp.add(keyPadPanel, BorderLayout.CENTER);
        cp.add(functionPanel, BorderLayout.EAST);
    }

    private class KeyPadButtonWatcher implements ActionListener
    {
        public void actionPerformed (ActionEvent a)
        {
            Object buttonPressed = a.getSource();
            if (buttonPressed.equals(keyPadButtons[0]))
            {
                currentDisplay = currentDisplay + "0";
                displayField.setText(currentDisplay);
            }
            if (buttonPressed.equals(keyPadButtons[1]))
            {
                currentDisplay = currentDisplay + "1";
                displayField.setText(currentDisplay);
            }
            if (buttonPressed.equals(keyPadButtons[2]))
            {
                currentDisplay = currentDisplay + "2";
                displayField.setText(currentDisplay);
            }
            if (buttonPressed.equals(keyPadButtons[3]))
            {
                currentDisplay = currentDisplay + "3";
                displayField.setText(currentDisplay);
            }
            if (buttonPressed.equals(keyPadButtons[4]))
            {
                currentDisplay = currentDisplay + "4";
                displayField.setText(currentDisplay);
            }
            if (buttonPressed.equals(keyPadButtons[5]))
            {
                currentDisplay = currentDisplay + "5";
                displayField.setText(currentDisplay);
            }
            if (buttonPressed.equals(keyPadButtons[6]))
            {
                currentDisplay = currentDisplay + "6";
                displayField.setText(currentDisplay);
            }
            if (buttonPressed.equals(keyPadButtons[7]))
            {
                currentDisplay = currentDisplay + "7";
                displayField.setText(currentDisplay);
            }
```

```
        if (buttonPressed.equals(keyPadButtons[8]))
        {
            currentDisplay = currentDisplay + "8";
            displayField.setText(currentDisplay);
        }
        if (buttonPressed.equals(keyPadButtons[9]))
        {
            currentDisplay = currentDisplay + "9";
            displayField.setText(currentDisplay);
        }
        if (buttonPressed.equals(pointButton))
        {
            currentDisplay = currentDisplay + ".";
            displayField.setText(currentDisplay);
        }
        if (buttonPressed.equals(clearButton))
        {
            currentDisplay = "";
            displayField.setText("0.0");
        }
    }
}

private class FunctionButtonWatcher implements ActionListener
{
    public void actionPerformed (ActionEvent a)
    {
        Object buttonPressed = a.getSource();
        if (buttonPressed.equals(addButton))
        {
            operand1 = currentDisplay;
            function = 1;
            currentDisplay = "";
            displayField.setText(currentDisplay);
        }
        if (buttonPressed.equals(subtractButton))
        {
            operand1 = currentDisplay;
            function = 2;
            currentDisplay = "";
            displayField.setText(currentDisplay);
        }
        if (buttonPressed.equals(multiplyButton))
        {
            operand1 = currentDisplay;
            function = 3;
            currentDisplay = "";
            displayField.setText(currentDisplay);
        }
```

```java
            if (buttonPressed.equals(divideButton))
            {
                operand1 = currentDisplay;
                function = 4;
                currentDisplay = "";
                displayField.setText(currentDisplay);
            }
        }
    }
    private class EqualsButtonWatcher implements ActionListener
    {
        public void actionPerformed (ActionEvent a)
        {
            switch (function)
            {
                case 1:
                {
                    result = Double.parseDouble(operand1) +
                            Double.parseDouble(currentDisplay);
                    displayField.setText("" + result);
                }
                break;
                case 2:
                {
                    result = Double.parseDouble(operand1) -
                            Double.parseDouble(currentDisplay);
                    displayField.setText("" + result);
                }
                break;
                case 3:
                {
                    result = Double.parseDouble(operand1) *
                            Double.parseDouble(currentDisplay);
                    displayField.setText("" + result);
                }
                break;
                case 4:
                {
                    result = Double.parseDouble(operand1) /
                            Double.parseDouble(currentDisplay);
                    displayField.setText("" + result);
                }
            }
        }
    }
}
```

Index